"REVOLUTION" should be redefined

Alex Ndukwe

Copyright © 2019 by Alex Ndukwe

All rights reserved

This book or any portion thereof may not be reproduced or used without the express written permission of the publisher except for the use of brief quotations in a book review

First printing, 2019

Printed in the united states of America

ISBN: 978-0-359-84094-6

Forward

The word revolution is a wonderful word and we need to understand it could be used positively to connote repair, improvements, revamping, create a positive bottom line etc.

We need to redefine it and ensure we don't allow the retrogressive, negative side of it that leads to violence, shedding of blood, destroy of infrastructure, removal of government. Let's weigh the options we have, our problem in Nigeria can be traced from first republic and we must begin to think of industrial revolution, Agricultural revolution, manufacturing revolution.

We have the potential of becoming the food basket of the world, industrial giant of the world and most importantly overtake china and other Asian tiger, the revolution would involve all sectors for this to happen.

An end to destruction, fight, deaths , disturbance of public peace etc. , rather let us join our hands together and revolutionize Nigeria positively and transit to 'Jerusalem of mecca' of industrialization and become exporters of goods and services, this revolution is possible, we must be ready to fall in line.

Table of Contents

Introduction

Chapter 1

The word Revolution

Chapter 2

A redefinition

Chapter 3

Rebranding for Results

Chapter 4

What's is your Stand

Dedication

Dr Goodluck Ebele Jonathan, Former president, Federal Republic of Nigeria, a man of peace and high moral standards.

'Revolution' should be redefined

Introduction

Mentioning this word 'revolution' sends a message and it's the drum of war, forceful removal of a government in power, this will lead to shedding of blood, decline in prosperity of the nation, destruction of existing infrastructures and severe poverty will be inflicted upon the nation and we must be wise as citizens of this great nation, Nigeria.

My voice would not be a lone voice in the wilderness, I believe many people share the same view with me , violence is not the best approach to resolving issues , good enough we have identified our problems and we need to proffer solutions and I believe you don't need to be a card carrying member of any political party to offer suggestion, either is adopted or rejected , it's on record you gave an advise on the way forward & history will bear witness of this fact when situations of things start to degenerate.

A typical example is one of our challenges , 'Banditry & kidnapping' , the Oni of Ife , Iku baba yeye, Oba Ogunwusi left the comfort of his palace to pay courtesy visit to President Buhari in Aso villa , solutions was proffered on using Technology to curb the menace in the south west, they suggested the use of drones, asked for approval so that it would be deployed immediately & President Buhari mentioned that CCTV will be installed on our high ways , these are suggestions and more ideas can be brought to the table.

I agree that civil societies are visible in any democratic dispensation any where in the world and also an important component in democratization , they often play the role of a watch dog, this should not be a licence for violence , arson, destabilizing peace in the society and there should be a drift from blame culture , I remember , 'Ali must Go' crises in 1977 , a high rise building was destroyed along Ikorodu road because of protest and we must not allow this happen , 'Bring Back our Girls' protest did you hear that anyone was killed , they pressed for their demand , the FGN swang into action and these girls were released and other movements should borrow a leaf from this movement , an end to destruction of life and property in the name of protest.

Historically we cannot divulge violence from revolution , we must redefine it , this is due to the fact that it's very expensive to replace damaged infrastructures , lives that are lost as a result of this revolt cannot be replaced , confidence of our potential foreign investors would decline and would require more efforts to convince them that our environment is save, educational system would be destabilized, we can keep on counting the demerits of this action , we need to put sentiments behind and face the reality.

We must not give up on project fix Nigeria , our little contribution is required for things to improve , I remember vividly the last redeem Parish I pastored and I altered the order of service , 'Opening prayer' and 'Intercession For Nigeria' meant different things , someone asked me,

'Revolution' should be redefined

'Pastor why and my response we need to pray for our country, Leadership, for God to help us' , that's a concerned pastor of a local church, he believes that peace must reign in his country before other things can follow, let's have a mind set that is positive, rather be an Agent of change and not an agent of destruction & crises.

Our Religious Leaders must be careful of what they preach, on no account should you incite your followers , Abuse the government of the day, make negative remarks , compare leaders etc. , see your role as a nation builder, you cannot destroy when you are a builder, God bless Nigeria.

The United Nations defines community development as "a process where community members come together to take collective action and generate solutions to common problems." It is a broad concept, applied to the practices of civic leaders, activists, involved citizens, and professionals to improve various aspects of communities, typically aiming to build stronger and more resilient local communities.

We need to take a closer look at our communities and don't depend on government all the time.

'Revolution' should be redefined

Chapter 1
....
Redefinition

"If every citizen can get rid of indiscipline syndrome, we have immense potential to build more productive, conflict-free, harmonious and peaceful communities, societies, cities, nations and world."

— Vishwas Chavan

There is need to redefine 'Revolution' in our hearts, let's ascribe positive meaning to this word , what it should stand for is resolution of our challenges , Technology and expertise should be adopted to see that a new dawn in terms of improvements in our society, we cannot run away from this challenges but we must take the bull by the horn & ensure positive change is attained.

"Rwanda Standards Board (RSB) has kicked-off a one-week awareness campaign on gradual transition from electricity and information technology to high-end technologies and use of Robotics in people's daily lives."

'Revolution' should be redefined

Organizers of this campaign want institutions to emulate some examples that are introducing 4th industrial revolution to Rwanda.

Those includes use of drones in agriculture, case of soil mapping and in health, case of medical delivery.4IR is high end technologies and trends which includes; Internet of things (IoT), robotics, virtual reality (VR) and artificial intelligence (AI) which are changing the way we live and work.

Private sector is also involved in this initiative , let us stop fighting the government of the day , some technocrats sold this idea to the government of Namibia and efforts are already in top gear to get it implemented. Our textile industries is dead and we need to resuscitate it, only CBN is making efforts , what of Manufacturers association of Nigeria , have they made any input? , we need to look for ways to resolve our problems and having it in mind that there is no need to blame anyone for these challenges, we have neglected technologies that are available in the world today.

What gives birth to policies is advise and inputs from experts , technocrats in chosen fields, you might say , they won't listen to me, give the advice first and leave the rest.

Sowore and his team should understand that the piper dictates the tune , the frustration here is not more than the fact that the appointees as ministers are party members of the ruling party , this is what I believe led to this cry of 'things are not working' , this trend is very peculiar in our polity and we cannot blame president Buhari , he has been under intense pressure from his party lobbyist before the list came out, imagine Ambode's name was not on the final list and other parties expected a national government , our democracy is still evolving and we will get there someday and we should not destroy our country with our bare hands and I'm really disappointed with the tweet I saw not quite long,

Revolutionary Olusegun Retweeted

'Revolution' should be redefined

Revolutionary Towolawi Jamiu

@jharmo

Whenever they try to teach us what democracy is, tell them we know those that fought for this democracy because their clueless ethnic tyrant was the one that overthrew a Democratic government.

#freesoworenow

#RevolutionNow

Let's return to our main focus in this chapter and forget insinuations on what led to the purported revolution , redefinition of this word must connote smoothing positive, we are aware that challenges in Nigeria has been revolving and most times we fold our arms and watch the government , accuse the leaders of not doing enough, as I pointed in one of my books which will soon be published , governments all over the world have little resources at their disposal , we need to understand this fact , they can be enablers for this change, someone has to initiate first and this is the issue we must visualize critically , the problem of 'banditry & insurgence' , is peculiar in states like borno, Zamfara , Adamawa and the use of the military force is a good initiative but we need to look are our borders , they are too porous , what efforts are we making to seal our borders and install a tight security around there , this accounts for reasons why this war cannot end in these areas.

We cannot blame the government , banditry had existed in these localities for a long time , it appears it has gotten out of hand now , before PMB's government we have had banditry on the outskirts of Sokoto town, I remember vividly when I had to visit the site at Sokoto for my former employers , I wore my corporate identity card on my neck and someone advised me to put it in my pocket, this happened when my driver stopped at a filling station at Damaturu to buy fuel , according to this fellow , bandits come from chad and they could attack without notice , though local vigilante group have been assisting to a larger extent.

Porous border is an issue, the need by our government to liaise with neighbouring countries in this respect can help to check illegal migrants gaining access, the border should be sealed immediately.

Herdsmen carrying weapons are not Nigerians, but illegal migrants from neighbouring countries, immigrations should step-up and ensure they checkmate movements around our borders, I want to appreciate some journalists they have made efforts to study the situation in this area and not quite long that I realised that there are two boko haram factions, the one on the outskirts of baga road happens to be very deadly, they have killed many of our soldiers and they are very close to the border town, our security operatives should think of using technology to win this war, reports from one of the TV news stations, they indicated that the terrorist move with mechanics, vulcanizers, other supports when they are in operations and all the vehicles of Nigerian army that are abandoned as a result of faults , they repair these cars and put them into use.

This war has been on for a while and we must access the situation, if we cannot fight this war effectively, at this point we should adopt other strategies that will help us make progress , I must confess the government of the day is doing it's best in terms of acquisition of weapons for our military & the Airforce have also assisted in bombing these terrorists.

Dissemination of information, it's a fact that some elements in our military give information to the terrorist and this must be curbed & it's not in our interest and this accounts for difficulty in killing these terrorists, when they receive information they relocate , though this claim in the media cannot be authenticated.

The locals in such environment should assist in providing information to the security agencies , it's a fact that some community leaders align with the enemies of the state , the locals should learn to blow the whistle immediately there is a threat , I'm aware the local vigilante groups have supported in this war, they must be very faithful in this fight, what is the need of leaving your communities and start residing at IDP camps , they need to be transparent in this war against terror , in Kano the insurgence did not last, whenever strange people emerge in the environment, the security agencies are involved , after a little while these attacks varnished. I received a call from the Group Head, Human resources that my staff at Kano had been arrested by SARs and my support is required for his release , little did I know that Group head, Kano region refused to get involved, I tried to find out and he told me he cannot do anything because of the nature of the case, I can't blame him. I started to think of the next line of action, I remembered our internal control staff was an ex-military officer and I got him on the phone and asked for help and he promised me that he will go to SARS office, most of those officers are his friend and he got there and he got details of what transpired, someone arrived from Kaduna to visit my staff and he got to his street and could not remember his surname and the locals considered him a boko haram suspect, they blew the whistle and he was arrested and my staff went to seek for his bail and they also arrested him. Can we see that security is everybody's business and we there is need for cooperation and ensure suspicious movements are reported , this helped to fight this war at Kano and I recall on Sundays , Muslims come to check on churches and ensure they are comfortable , there was maximum cooperation and this should be the case in North East.

Conducts of the locals matter a lot in this war that is ongoing, they must not connive, rather they MUST expose these bad elements to appropriate quarters immediately.

I'm positive that our military can win this war, let us not lose sleep over this.

Definitely my views are balanced, I'm not a card carrying member of any political party, we need to tell ourselves the truth, PMB cannot be blamed for some of these issues , Nigeria is suffering from failed Leadership since the first republic , let's stop complaining and see how we can salvage the situation, the current government is doing a lot now but the effect might not be felt immediately, let's embrace revolution in Agriculture , according to PMB a country with a population of 200 million people , it's not practical to import food rather we should feed ourselves , I want to challenge professionals in the private sector, how many of us own farms of our own, let's think of subsistence, I want to encourage us , you might not need to carry hoe and cutlass but engage labourers , this will create jobs , though it's an informal sector and I want to share with us that the unemployment rate in Thailand is 1% , though I agree it might be a seasonal thing , we should change our mentality, during the last salah break , we visited our family friend and behold at the back of their house is a small poultry farm , 6 drums with cart fish, small house for livestock like goats , rams etc , let's assume every Nigerian family can engage in this , our story can improve , there is bound to be excess supply compared to demand and prices can come down , this is another kind of revolution, what do you think.

Agriculture is a big business in some countries like united states, Britain , Thailand, Malaysia etc , revenues are generated from exports and we can do the same here , let's learn from the Rice revolution and once more kudos to PMB for this and we have been able to save billions of naira in imports of this commodity , now some African countries have come to learn from us in this revolution of rice farming.

I read in the news of ban on imported milk, let us focus on all aspect of agriculture, procure machinery for processing and stop wasting hard currencies on import, this can move us out of poverty as a nation.

I'm quite delighted that private sector, banks are getting involved with agriculture, not only because risk assets are tied to it, but want to ensure that the sector improves and grow quickly, lot of wealth is embedded in it.

'Revolution' should be redefined

Rural areas in Nigeria are neglected and abandoned , NGO's are doing a lot at the moment their attention is more focused on the communities in the north east and other LGA should be supported, I'm fully aware of road projects in some oil producing areas been handled by NDDC , other communities should benefit , apart from infrastructures we should also look at machinery for agriculture processing , I know the pain some farmers in this area encounter with processing of their farm produce , like garri production , private sector should wade into this matter, storage and processing equipment's will also help our economy as well, waste of these produce will be eliminated, we need revolution in this area , it's a good thing that local governments are now receiving FAC allocation , LGA government should not embezzle such funds, look in wards into your communities and ensure machinery are provided and this will rub on your communities.

'Revolution' should be redefined

We appreciate God for some firms in the private sector that engage in corporate responsibility projects in major cities in Nigeria, they need to revolutionize by extending such gestures to the rural communities , this should be beyond cleaning the environments, rather think of a project that could be executed in such communities, I know we most times business minded , some school of thought will start thinking of what they will benefit , I want to advise that this should be in line with agriculture , training that will empower the farmers in terms of skills that will boost production in commodities , FGN has already subsidized the cost of fertilizers , some farmers still cannot afford to buy, efforts could be made in this area. Rural electrification , some communities are on the grid but still experience stable power , what will it cost to install a mini solar electrification plant , 10 corporate bodies with common business interest can come together and execute such projects and this is the kind of revolution we want to see happen , Governor Ishaku granted interview on need to make the

'Revolution' should be redefined

Mambila plateau a tourist attraction, by building access road atop the hills, this is a good opportunity for the private sector to partner with the state and make it a tourist attraction for people all over the world, it's the coolest place in Nigeria. Nigerian citizens in diaspora are not left out in this arrangement.

Community development seeks to empower individuals and groups of people with the skills they need to effect change within their communities. These skills are often created through the formation of social groups working for a common agenda. Community developers must understand both how to work with individuals and how to affect communities' positions within the context of larger social institutions.

We have always spoken about the mineral resources untapped & unexploited in Nigeria and I get sick when I hear people in the media speak of government assistance to help with the mining, there's a limit with respect to such involvement, can't the private sector invest in this area,

'Revolution' should be redefined

especially minerals that could serve as raw materials for our local industry, we should not forget that we need an industrial revolution and this is a path to such achievements and I would like us to pay attention to this , Nigerian banks should wake up and become an agent of change, rather than handle short time investments with higher return, reviving our dead industries is a major challenge in our economy and we can take up this challenge, CBN took a bold step on our textile industry looking at ways of revamping it, in logical terms I can say CBN have indeed taken steps to revolutionize some dead sectors , at first Rice production , it's a success as far as I'm concerned.

Revolutionizing our society is beyond shedding blood and attempting to destabilise the government of the day , let us look at how we can be agent of the next level , during the nations cup in 2013 , Late coach Steven Keshi's team was not given any chance and they won the championship , he had issues with NFF and ask me

'Revolution' should be redefined

what was the issue? , the federation could not provide him with an official car and an accommodation, Chief Mike Adenuga was in south Africa for other engagements and watched the final at FNB stadium , after the match , apart from the fact that he was proud to be a Nigerian, he showered the team with cash gifts and he had an interaction with Keshi and he discovered the needed to support him, the complaint was received by the mogul and he instructed his PA to arrange for 2 cars and an accommodation, this is revolution in sports, I know you might say Afterall he's a rich man, how many rich men in Nigeria are ready to render such support to their national teams, it's an example of a Nigerian that is engrossed in revolutionizing sports and this will ensure that our youths bring more glory to Nigeria , left for me I would say that corporate Nigeria should relief the FGN from funding sports , Sports is a big business all over the world , what will make Africans follow foreign football leagues like premiership , La Liga, Bundesliga , it's due to total involvement of the private sector and not their governments , government's role should not exceed providing frame work for operations and that's all and nothing more.

What of Captain Mikel Obi, another patriot , during the Olympic games , U-23 eagles was stranded and he paid the bills of this team which he also captained as one of the over aged players and the team picked up a bronze medal in Rio Olympics , this is what we are talking about, let us repair when the opportunity comes and we can do it , rather than create more problems , when they returned home everyone celebrated them an no one will ask a question of how bills were settled.

Dear reader I know the thoughts in our hearts will be that where do we get money to be involved in a positive minded revolution, that's not the idea of redefinition but rather we can make sure that we are agents to this agenda, there a lot of area that requires our involvement in our communities , when I was growing up , in our community , Ajose Street, Illasamaja, Lagos state we faced a challenge of intense robbery attacks and the residents agreed to form a vigilante group , my late father at that time was a Senior manager in Union bank joined the group and they provided security for our street and this incidence was curbed once and for all , this is what I'm saying , the residents came together and resolved their problems.

The only way you can remove a government is by election , wait for the next four years and I want to disagree with the human rights lawyers , they should stop encouraging acts that can throw our nation into a thick darkness and destruction that will take us many years to repair , we quite agree that the numbers are not what we want to see with respect to dictates in our economy and the deplorable conditions of the common man on the streets , we can make out the best from what we are seeing.

'Revolution' should be redefined

The time is now for us to redefine revolution in our hearts and success will be attained and we can reclaim our position as giant of Africa.

Chapter 3
Rebranding for Results

"The development of science has produced an industrial revolution which has brought different peoples in such close contact with one another through colonization and commerce that no matter how some nations may still look down upon others, no country can harbour the illusion that its career is decided wholly within itself."

John Dewey (1916)

We need to understand the concept of rebranding before we proceed with this chapter with respect to the burning issue at hand.

It's assumed of the existence of a brand, an improvement for market penetration, acceptance would lead to success been recorded and profit soars to the peak, that's the meaning of Rebranding , it involves a lot of things like repackaging , strategies like making smaller packs for the low income consumer etc

Nigeria is like a brand that is peculiar in nature , with over 250 ethnic groups and 520 languages spoken , in my other book, 'Our nation can be

'Revolution' should be redefined

great' , I did mention that our country is not a mistake but a perfect design made in heaven by Almighty God, but we must not forget that it's how we handle this brand that matters and would determine success that we can achieve or attain.

It's not uncommon for government of the day to make frantic efforts to project the Nigerian brand oversees to woo foreign investors and ensure a positive impact is felt in our economy and we must not dislocate these efforts by our negative actions , VP Osinbajo has been active in this pursuit and we need to commend the ruling government for these efforts.

We need to understand that , our dear nation requires a total rebranding that cuts across all levels and we are all a component of this exercise and we must pay attention to my comments on this issue , though it might not be palatable to us, truth is definitely bitter.

We need to co-exists and bond with ourselves , have you noticed the power of football whenever Nigeria is participating in a tournament just like the

'Revolution' should be redefined

AFCON 2019, I call it a special religion, it has the unifying power to bring people of diverse cultures together, everyone is monitoring the round leather been kicked around and when it enters the net of the opponent, there will emerge a great shout, 'GOAL!!!!' and the fans embrace themselves & rejoicing pumps up in the air and this should be our attitude when we are not watching football, despite the diverse language we now speak & understand the language of football.

Our attitude in our country in terms of relationship with one another will make the whole world see us as a country that is peaceful, this would improve our rating to the outside world, we need to accommodate the inadequacies of one another, we are people with diverse cultures and we cannot judge ourselves with our own expectations, we need to support one another for a great brand called Nigeria and I will give an examples, please I'm a detribalised citizen, my parents are from the east and I was born and raised in the west and I spent my youthful age working in

'Revolution' should be redefined

Northern Nigeria , let's continue our discussion, the Fulani headers live a nomadic life and this involve moving with their life stocks from place to place , it's rather unfortunate that some of us do not understand this , I personally agree with the RUGA initiative of FGN , because it's the way forward and this will prevent clashes with farmers nationwide , we need to understand with this Fulani's , they are Nigerians and they should have the freedom of movement anywhere in Nigeria , I'm shocked to see agitation from some people that FG should not implement grazing reserves and some state governments are not in support , we need to come together as a nation and allow this implementation , the merits is that our food production in the rural areas that are on the decline since the clashes started since last year would take an upward swing.

I lived in Kano for 16 years and I also know the culture around there too and relationship with strangers , it should also improve and I don't care terminologies of yamari or berebe , we cannot change the culture of an ethnic group , they have been like that, we should respect their culture and co-exist as friends and partners in progress and live in peace and it might interest you that Yoruba's live in the enclave of the Hausa's called city , we must adopt the football mentality across all levels.

The rebranding of Nigeria is in our hands, image laundering might not be 100% effective, our behavioural patterns will help us a great deal, let us love ourselves, we are one and nothing should separate us.

We should be free to do business anywhere in Nigeria , move freely and I remember Umuofia , an Igbo man established a tomatoes paste factory at Sokoto state , the government gave him land and cooperated with this investor and they did not chase him away because he's yamiri , he came with a venture that created employment and emergence of a Nigerian product, this gesture from that state government should be emulated by others and we should end tribalism.

'Revolution' should be redefined

Let's look at another angle , if you check publications released by U.S department of states , they inform their citizens not to visit some countries but in our case they indicates states in Nigeria that are not save and their citizens should not go to such places and I want to challenge the locals, what efforts are you making to ensure there is an improvement , agreed the FGN have deployed troops to these locations and results are yet to come, I'm not saying you should carry weapons and fight but cooperate with the security agencies in terms of providing information about the movement of the terrorist and community leaders should not aid these terrorist no matter the threat issued by them. The war against these terrorist must be supported by the locals , if there's peace in their localities , businesses will flourish , the last time I visited Maiduguri and my driver took me to the fish market and what I saw was not encouraging, it looked deserted , I wept in my heart. The need to prevent our children & wards to be recruited by this terrorist and this will ensure they don't have accessories they will use to perpetuate this crime to humanity. The locals should ensure they frustrate the operations of these people as much as possible. Though we commend the creation of civilian JTF during the trying period in North east, it helped the soldiers in the war because these are locals they understand the terrain and our communities should more of this in the fight of the war. Though is a very tough task considering the environments involved considering the nearness of these communities to the border of some countries that make the infiltration of these enemies possible as well as their escape. These challenges are noted but the locals should not be discouraged in the required task ahead. FGN is not relenting in their efforts in this war, the locals need to support the soldiers with information's where necessary.

Religious tolerance , this is another important aspect to peace in our nation, I can say there is improvement and it can get better , there is no need to talk against ourselves or condemn believes of others , within the same religion we are likely to see different groups , we need to respect ourselves and enthrone peace and unity , we have had matasine riots in 1982 , 1995 riots in kano against Christians and this has not happened in recent times. We need to respect ourselves avoid attacks and assaults against believes of others.

It is a known phenomenon that many of us reside in major cities in Nigeria and our roots are traced to a rural communities and we must not neglect these communities , efforts should be made to improve quality of lives in these places and this appeal is to government of the day, individuals , corporate bodies, public sector etc. , we need to ensure that we empower the youths of these communities to be productive and not be turned to accessories to crime , most of these youths in the rural area are not employed , empowerment is not to provide shoe shinning kit for these youths , rather there is need to draft empower programmes that will improve their life and also make them useful to themselves and their society. We need to look into this , the campaign should encourage them to return back to the farm , relevant agencies should look into this ,national orientation agency should handle this effectively by running a campaign in these localities with cooperation from there perspective state governments , it will be a thing of joy if the youths in these localities are actively engaged , tools for crime will be very limited or not even available for use.

We need to commend the government of the day with the new agreement signed with siemens on power , there's need for us to eliminate waste of resources and focus on reducing the infrastructure gaps in our society , this will speed up our industrialization drive to a greater extent and the rural communities should not be left out, appreciations for some subsidies that have been implemented and more is expected in Agriculture so as to boost this sector and make our country self sufficient in food production and earn foreign exchange.

Chapter 4

....
What is your stand?

"I like to see a man proud of the place in which he lives. I like to see a man live so that his place will be proud of him."

Abraham Lincoln

Looking at chapter 2 and 3 of this book, what is your view and are you ready for the wind of change that will take us to the next level, there an urgent need to change our mentality so as to enable us fall into line.

I mentioned definition of revolution in our hearts and this will help us as a nation, let's think of this word in terms of improving areas in our lives that requires revival and we mentioned some few sailing points.

Taste for foreign goods, once we embrace local contents, this will have a positive effect on our indigenous firm, we are all guilty of this and we must change, why buy fabrics from abroad, cars from overseas when we have local assembly plants, buy Thailand rice when we have our own home grown rice, go for medical tourism when these treatments can be done locally, I'm glad that diary products will soon be added to the prohibitive list of importation and this will boost our local diary firms in Nigeria.

When we curtail our taste it helps to grow our local firms and ensure the smugglers are out of business, since no one will patronize them, as citizens of Nigeria we need not to be forced but we should decide to cooperate and ensure we improve the lots of our local firms.

Thank God you are a professional, let me ask you a simple question, what is your contribution to nation building in your immediate community, I believe you have a good answer, it should not be less than ensuring you deploy your expertise in developing your community, a medical doctor should be ready to organise medical outreach in his/her community when celebrating a birthday, instead of spending on throwing party, why don't you touch lives with the little resources you would have wasted for the belly of many individuals , it's a suggestion don't forget the newly elected law maker from Lagos state , he paid lesson fee for 2,000 pupils in his local government for summer coaching , let us emulate people like this and we will be seen as contributing our little quota in various direction.

As we make progress in our vocation, career we must have it at the back of our minds of what we can do for our country and not what our country can always do for us .

Shun tribalism , see your composite tribe as a friends and not an enemy, cooperate with them to make things better in the community you find yourself, ensuring we are positive and focused, be ready to make impacts on people's lives , refuse to be a complainant , be an agent of change , make your impact to be felt wherever you find yourself.

A set of values and practices which plays a special role in overcoming poverty and disadvantage, knitting society together at the grass roots and deepening democracy. There is a community development profession, defined by national occupational standards and a body of theory and experience going back the best part of a century. There are active citizens who use community development techniques on a voluntary basis, and there are also other professions and agencies which use a community development approach or some aspects of it

We should support our government and not to castigate them , resources are very limited all over the world , most times our leaders have to struggle with raising funds to implement our budgets and to build & maintain already existing infrastructures in the country , we must understand this.

Refuse to be an accessory to demonstrations, this should not be viewed as revolution but destruction to life's and properties, tacking us to dark ages and we must refuse to participate in such moves.

Among comity of nations , sports bring glory and also wealth and I want to challenge our ex-footballers , athletes etc. what is their involvement in nurturing future stars , we need to note that efforts can be made by building football academy where young people can be nurtured and this should not affect their education , with facilities that are state of the art compared to what is obtainable in Europe and America , already we have existing structures and these efforts can be augmented by their efforts , they should give back to their society that made them what they are today.

Alternatively these stars can come together and put up standard facilities that will help improve the sports and bring glory to our father land and wealth , they could organize coaching clinics , serve as ambassadors for the game and inspire the up coming athletes, it's a good approach that some of these ex-sportsmen/women are involved in sports administration in various state governments and will also help.

There is an urgent need to revolutionaries all sectors of our economy and ensure we make impacts that can be felt and seen worldwide, very

'Revolution' should be redefined

soon citizens of other countries will start scrambling for Nigerian Visa just like the way we scramble for theirs and these is achievable.

'Revolution' should be redefined

www.ingramcontent.com/pod-product-compliance
Lightning Source LLC
Chambersburg PA
CBHW032007060426
42449CB00032B/1183